JLS
ANOTHER BEAT

POSY EDWARDS

Introduction

Boyband JLS, Aston Merrygold, Marvin Humes, Jonathan 'JB' Gill, and Oritsé Williams wowed viewers and the judges on 2008's *The X Factor* right from their first audition. 'These boys could really win it!' Simon Cowell whispered to the other judges as the boys passed their first audition with flying colours. But despite making it all the way to the final, the boys eventually came in a close second to competition winner Alexandra Burke.

Although this could have been the end of the road for JLS, that wasn't the case at all. Their shining talent and the hard work they put into the group paid off, and the boys eventually bagged two number one singles, a number one album that went platinum, and won two MOBO Awards for Best UK Newcomer and Best Song to boot!

But it's been a long and hard journey for Oritsé, Aston, Marvin and JB. Although it might have been *The X Factor* that catapulted them to fame, they almost didn't even enter the competition to begin with. Read on to get all the gossip on how the boys found each other, backstage whisperings from *The X Factor*, learn about their trendy style and fashion sense, and even share their date and love secrets!

oritsé

marvin

aston

jb

chapter 1
Meet The Boys!

'Everyday I have to pinch myself . . . This is closer than I ever could've imagined to the original idea for JLS.'
Oritse's dream has become a reality.

factbook Aston

| JLS | Aston | Marvin | JB | Oritsé |

What would you like to ask ASTON?

NAME – Aston Merrygold

BORN – 13th February 1988

HOMETOWN – Peterborough, England

STAR SIGN – Aquarius

EYE COLOUR – Brown

WHAT WAS YOUR NICKNAME AT SCHOOL? – Lil' Man, A.S.

FAVOURITE COLOUR – Blue

FAVOURITE FOOD – Tuna and Pasta or Pizza

FAVOURITE SPORT (to watch or to play) – Football

WHAT IS YOUR IDEAL WEEKEND? – Waking up late, partying all weekend

WHAT IS YOUR FAVOURITE HOLIDAY DESTINATION? – Florida, America

IF YOU WERE AN ANIMAL, WHAT WOULD YOU BE? – A cheetah or a little monkey

WHAT'S YOUR MOST EMBARRASSING MOMENT? – I don't really get embarrassed. I embarrass people!

TELL US ONE SECRET ABOUT YOU OR A FELLOW BAND MATE – JB likes to stand next to a window, look up on the horizon and put lotion on himself. HA!

WHAT WAS THE FIRST ALBUM YOU EVER BOUGHT? – Usher – *My Way*

WHAT IS THE BEST CONCERT YOU HAVE EVER ATTENDED? – Boyz II Men

factbook Marvin

JLS | Aston | Marvin | JB | Oritsé

What would you like to ask MARVIN?

NAME – Marvin Humes

BORN – 18th March 1985

HOMETOWN – Woolwich, England

STAR SIGN – Pisces

EYE COLOUR – Brown

FAVOURITE COLOUR – Green

FAVOURITE FOOD – Nando's

FAVOURITE SPORT (to watch or to play) – Football

WHAT'S ON YOUR IPOD? – Beyoncé – *I am … Sasha Fierce*

WHAT IS YOUR IDEAL WEEKEND? – Somewhere hot with beaches, cocktails, good shopping and great clubs!

WHAT IS YOUR FAVOURITE HOLIDAY DESTINATION? – Thailand

WHO ARE YOUR HEROES? – Martin Luther King, Michael Jackson, Mum and Dad

WHAT MAKES YOU LAUGH? – Adam Sandler movies and Eddie Murphy stand up

DO YOU PLAY ANY INSTRUMENTS? – A little piano!!

IF YOU WERE AN ANIMAL, WHAT WOULD YOU BE? – A lion

TELL US ONE SECRET ABOUT YOU OR A FELLOW BAND MATE – Aston lives on tomato ketchup – literally!

WHAT WAS THE FIRST ALBUM YOU EVER BOUGHT? – Michael Jackson – *Bad*

WHAT IS THE BEST CONCERT YOU HAVE EVER ATTENDED? – Michael Jackson – Dangerous 1994

HOME　　FRIENDS　　SEARCH

factbook JB

[JLS | Aston | Marvin | JB | Oritsé]

What would you like to ask JB?

NAME – Jonathan Benjamin Gill

BORN – 7th December 1986

HOMETOWN – Croydon, England

STAR SIGN – Sagittarius

EYE COLOUR – Brown

WHAT WAS YOUR NICKNAME AT SCHOOL? – Gilly, Gillster & JG

FAVOURITE COLOUR – Yellow

FAVOURITE FOOD – Chinese

FAVOURITE SPORT (to watch or to play) – Playing rugby and watching football

WHAT'S ON YOUR IPOD? – The Script

WHAT IS YOUR IDEAL WEEKEND? – Sleeping and Nando's

WHAT IS YOUR FAVOURITE HOLIDAY DESTINATION? – The Caribbean

WHAT MAKES YOU LAUGH? – Aston!!

DO YOU PLAY ANY INSTRUMENTS? – Yes, the flute and the piano

IF YOU WERE AN ANIMAL, WHAT WOULD YOU BE? – A koala

WHAT WAS THE FIRST ALBUM YOU EVER BOUGHT? – Backstreet Boys – *Backstreet's Back*

WHAT IS THE BEST CONCERT YOU HAVE EVER ATTENDED? – Prince

HOME  FRIENDS SEARCH

factbook Oritsé

[JLS] [Aston] [Marvin] [JB] [Oritsé]

What would you like to ask ORITSE?

NAME – Oritsé Williams

BORN – 27th November 1986

HOMETOWN – Fulham, England

STAR SIGN – Sagittarius

EYE COLOUR – Hazel

WHAT WAS YOUR NICKNAME AT SCHOOL? – Glitzy Ritzy and Music Boy

FAVOURITE COLOUR – Red

FAVOURITE FOOD – Nando's

FAVOURITE SPORT (to watch or to play) – Table tennis. 'Ask Marvin about that, he'll let you know our match score to date'

WHAT'S ON YOUR IPOD? – Lauryn Hill – *The Miseducation of Lauryn Hill*

WHAT IS YOUR IDEAL WEEKEND? – A weekend in the Caribbean

WHAT IS YOUR FAVOURITE HOLIDAY DESTINATION? – The Caribbean

IF YOU WERE AN ANIMAL, WHAT WOULD YOU BE? – An eagle

TELL US ONE SECRET ABOUT YOU OR A FELLOW BAND MATE – JB needs a minimum of 8 hours sleep

WHAT IS YOUR BIGGEST AMBITION FOR THE FUTURE? – For JLS to become the biggest band in the world!

WHAT WAS THE FIRST ALBUM YOU BOUGHT? – Sisqó – *Unleash the Dragon*

WHAT IS THE BEST CONCERT YOU HAVE EVER ATTENDED? – Tina Turner

HOME  FRIENDS SEARCH

chapter 2

Life Before Fame

According to Marvin, the name JLS came from the group's British identity. 'Jack the Lad Swing' was a combination of the New Jack Swing (an American genre that groups like Jodeci and Boyz II Men belonged to), and the boys' own cheeky charm.

★ JLS

The Dream

Although JLS came to be one of the best loved and most successful boybands of the decade, people only found out about the group through 2008's *The X Factor*. In reality, the JLS dream started years before that as the bright idea of a young Oritsé, who was studying at university in London in 2007.

He had always been musical as a child, and while at university he had been thinking about launching a career as a solo R&B artist. However, when Take That re-united, he realised there was a gap in the market for a young boyband, and decided to form one.

Family First

But Oritsé's motivation was personal as well as musical. He wanted to earn some money for his mum Sonia who suffers from multiple sclerosis. Oritsé's family had suffered some very hard times, and he was determined to raise cash to help pay for her treatments.

Looking For Talent

When he began the hunt for other members of the group, Oritsé spread the search as far as he could. The ambitious singer started looking through hundreds of MySpace pages of local talent, and placed adverts in music shops all over London's West End. Yet it was recommendations from his friends that eventually contributed to the group's final line up: Aston, JB, and Marvin.

A friend of Oritsé's put him in touch with Marvin, who he arranged to meet in London's Oxford Circus. Thinking that there was no time like the present, Oritsé decided to audition Marvin right there in the middle of the street. Fortunately for him, Marvin was a born performer, and wasted no time in singing his heart out, even pulling a few dance moves that made passers-by cheer him!

another beat ★

The Dream Team

Marvin already knew Aston, who he met at an audition for a TV advert. When Oritsé told Marvin he was still looking for members, Marvin handed over his mobile with Aston's number, and told Oritsé he had to call him, right then and there. The group was almost complete – they just needed one more future superstar to create the magic number of four. And the second Oritsé met JB he knew that his charisma and charm meant he would fit in perfectly.

Before Oritsé finalised his dream team, he sat for hours, pouring through all the potential group members he had met. He put photographs of different boys next to each other, working out the group dynamic, seeing what combination worked. But as soon as he put his photograph next to Marvin, Aston and JB, it was magic. He knew he had found the secret formula!

★ JLS

The Next Step

Immediately after the group formed, they felt a special bond with each other. Oritsé opened up to the boys about his tough home life. Instantly, the other three said they would always look out for him.

The four were soon devoting all their spare time to rehearsing at a dance studio in London's West End. They began playing gigs around London, though often they'd come away with less than £50 for their night's work. But it didn't matter – they knew that the hard work they put in and all the practice would pay off in the end. So they put plenty of thought into how they sounded as a group – and how they looked.

Keeping up the Studies

Although they were serious about the group, they also knew how few bands actually made it, so they were all working and studying hard outside the studio, just in case. Oritsé was studying events management, JB was studying theology, and Marvin was a property developer. But as it started looking like they had a chance of a serious shot at the music industry, they became less interested in their studies.

another beat ★

The X Factor

Friends and families of the boys began suggesting they take the group to try out for *The X Factor*. At a band meeting, the boys discussed whether they thought it was a good idea or not. They didn't want to try out, thinking that they could get there with their effort and determination alone.

But – even though things were going well for the band – they talked and talked about it, then made a group decision to try out for *The X Factor*. Things were looking good for the group anyway – so if they didn't get through, they would just carry on. After all, what did they have to lose?

chapter 3

The X Factor

'If you'd asked us who we wanted to guide us, we might have said Simon, or Cheryl, as she was a new judge. But luckily for us, as it turned out, we had Louis. Remember the success he's had with Westlife, Boyzone and even Girls Aloud in the early stages. He worked really hard for us … he got quite emotional!'
JB

★ JLS

Band from the Start

From day one, JLS had something that set them apart from almost every other group that had auditioned for *The X Factor*. They were already a real group. They hadn't just formed for the competition – they had been singing and dancing together for over a year, and formed a brotherly bond that worked hugely in their favour.

'At the auditions, when we were lining up to see the judges, everything was going wrong,' Oritsé remembers. 'JB had cut his hand on glass, Aston was desperate for the toilet, Marvin was the most nervous I'd ever seen him, and I was the same. When we went in, I was thinking: "You know, this can go totally wrong . . ." We saw Simon sighing, with his head in his hands, and we thought he was going to hate us. But thankfully we had a good start and that set us up!'

As Louis Walsh had to mentor the groups in the competition, JLS were relying on his knowledge and experience with groups to steer them to victory. But just two weeks into the show, JLS were Louis's last remaining act in the competition. To try and get some public support behind the boyband, Louis walked the streets of London in a bright green JLS hoodie, handing out flyers and asking people to support JLS!

Saved by Simon!

But the boys showed they were more than capable of making pop gold out of a number of different styles of music. Although they gave tight performances of tracks like *I'll Make Love to You* by Boyz II Men, *The Way You Make Me Feel* by Michael Jackson, *Ain't That a Kick in the Head?* by Dean Martin, *Baby One More Time* by Britney Spears (and other songs by Mariah Carey, The Beatles, The Isley Brothers and Take That), they were sometimes criticised by the judges for making poor decisions in their music choice.

As Aston sings many of the group's lead vocals, he would blame himself if things went badly on the show. On a few occasions, Oritsé had to run after him and tell him to pull himself together. 'Aston – we can get through this if we deliver a phenomenal second performance.'

This led to them finishing in the bottom two in week seven, but they were saved by the judges after Simon Cowell told the boys they didn't deserve to be at the bottom of the list. They went on to the semi-finals of the competition, in a nail-biting finale that had the nation on the edge of its seat!

★ JLS

Fans' Favourite

As if being in the competition wasn't stressful enough, the boys had drama surrounding them away from *The X Factor* studios. At a free show in Surrey, nearly 3,000 screaming fans turned up to watch JLS. However, when the venue filled up, disappointed fans rushed forwards, trying to stampede inside to see their beloved JLS. People in the crowd even witnessed rival girl gangs in the crowd fighting!

It was a chaotic scene, but it hinted at how popular the boys had already become before the competition had even finished.

As the show approached the semi-final, JLS had decided to sing Rihanna's *Umbrella* – and were due to perform alongside princess Rihanna herself! But a matter of days before the final, Rihanna cancelled, sending all the contestants and the production crew into chaos.

It was a real mess up. JLS – who had been extremely confident about their performance – were suddenly worried that they couldn't prepare enough. But they didn't show it onstage. The boys gave such strong performances that even Simon Cowell said to them: 'I'm gonna make a prediction, you could actually win this competition!' JLS ended up with the most votes in the semi-final, sailing through to the final.

'We work hard. That's our ethos. It's important to do things properly. JLS is all about excellence!'
JB

another beat

Finals Time!

If the semi-final was stressful to watch, the final was a million times worse! All around the country, devoted JLS fans were glued to their TVs, watching their boys team up with Westlife to sing their hit single *Flying Without Wings*. They watched as the boys managed to get through the first public vote (which saw Eoghan Quigg voted off). The boys then performed their own version of *Hallelujah*, but in the second public vote that night, Alexandra Burke came out on top, with JLS coming in second, only the fourth group ever to make the final on the show.

As gracious and respectful as ever – even in defeat – the boys immediately surrounded Alex and congratulated her on her win.

Though they were disappointed not to have won, they had no time to mope. *The X Factor* tour was about to set off around the UK, and the boys were about to show everyone exactly what they were made of. The JLS steam train was just about to pick up some steam!

chapter 4

Beyond The X Factor

'I never thought we would be here! I never thought we'd get nominated, and I never thought we would win two awards!'
Marvin on winning two MOBOs.

★ JLS

Although Alexandra Burke had won *The X Factor*, it seemed increasingly as if JLS were winners too. As *The X Factor* tour played to sold out arenas around the UK, crowds of screaming fans turned out to cheer JLS on. The boys sang a handful of Michael Jackson's hits, and with their soulful harmonies, slick moves and good looks, they were a smash hit.

Rumours circulated that the boys were jealous of the star treatment that Alex was receiving on the road, but they knew that was just the media trying to stir up trouble. In reality they were grateful to be getting the exposure that they were on the tour. 'The show opened up so many doors for you that you didn't even know existed before,' said Marvin. 'Without that platform it would've taken us much longer to get to where we are now.'

Record Contract Beckons . . .

Part of that was hooking up with Epic Records' Managing Director, Nick Raphael, who was the man behind stars like Lemar and Jay-Z. Although rumour had it that Simon Cowell's record company, Syco, was set to sign the boys, that deal fell through, and JLS found themselves signed to Epic Records.

The boys worked super hard on their music and their performances at Epic,

another beat

and they were rewarded in July 2009 when their debut single *Beat Again* went straight in at number one, and sold 100,000 copies in a week – becoming the fastest selling debut single of the year!

Instead of blowing a load of cash on a lavish party, they decided to celebrate in a more low-key way. Aston spills, 'When we had a party to celebrate reaching No. 1 in the charts, we went to Tesco and bought champagne on a buy-one-get-one-free deal and took it back to mine!'

Supporting a Hero

Riding on the wave of popularity since appearing on *The X Factor*, the boys spent the summer playing a number of big shows around the UK. However, their biggest thrill came when R&B soul star Lemar asked the boys to support him on his tour. Lemar had noticed the boyband on *The X Factor*, and had been really impressed with their performances. JLS jumped at the chance of appearing on the road with one of their biggest heroes!

The tour definitely spread the JLS love to a much wider audience. And suddenly, before they knew it, there was even more good news – the boys had been nominated for two MOBO Awards! They were over the moon just to be nominated – but totally stunned to pick up not one, but both awards at the show, for Best Song with *Beat Again*, and Best Newcomer, beating *The X Factor* rival and pal, Alex Burke.

★ JLS

another beat

But JLS had no time to enjoy the win – they immediately returned to work, preparing for their 2010 tour, and releasing their second single. *Everybody in Love* not only went to number one in the singles chart but knocked Cheryl Cole off the top spot!

Riding High

They spent many months at work on their debut album, and were rewarded for their hard work when it went straight into the chart at number one, again knocking Cheryl Cole off the top spot and beating Robbie Williams. Not bad for a debut album!

However, it wasn't all good news. Disaster struck when thousands of screaming fans turned out to see the boys turn on the Christmas lights in Manchester. So many fans turned up that the entrance was completely blocked, meaning that JLS couldn't actually get into the building!

'We had to change in the car then go straight onto the red carpet. We never thought it would be anything like that. It was crazy,' says Aston. Thankfully no one was seriously hurt.

Back to their Roots

Following their chart success and growing popularity, Oritsé, Marvin, Aston and JB were invited back onto *The X Factor* to perform in the 2009 series, as the most successful group ever to graduate from the show.

When they returned to the set, it was just like the old days. In fact, the boys completely forgot to head to their own luxury performer's dressing room – and started heading for the contestants' dressing rooms instead! The boys eventually found where they were supposed to go, and got on stage to perform their second single *Everybody in Love*, to the sounds of wild screaming from the crowd. It was awesome! And it just went to show the huge phenomenon that JLS had become in just two short years!

chapter 5

Style & Looks

From day one, it wasn't just their smooth dance moves or killer harmonies that got us hooked on JLS. It was their unique group style and cheeky smiles too!

Although each of the boys likes to rock their own look, they also make sure they're wearing complimentary outfits when they perform onstage, and even when they're seen out on the town!

ASTON

Aston describes his own personal style as pure JLS – or 'Jents Looking Sick!'. He loves the colour grey, and although he doesn't have a favourite item of clothing, he's often seen rocking his trademark beanie. If you fancy catching Aston when he's out shopping, you can bet he'll be found in All Saints or Topman – his favourite high street shops!

'We're all equal – and there's no jealousy about Aston emerging as the focus of the group'
Oritsé

39

MARVIN

Marvin's favourite designer is Vivienne Westwood, and he can often be spotted sporting VW chains and other accessories. He describes his own personal style as 'cool, chilling, sophisticated, slick, and sweetboy!', and he likes wearing slinky fitting tops to show off that killer bod!

'I train as I believe it's part of the whole package: you've got to look good and feel good – plus it's nice for the ladies to see us at our peak,' says Marvin about the group's dedication to physical fitness.

41

JB

JB loves a nice fitting leather jacket, and says that his style is 100 per cent pure 'Urban Gentleman'. Although he's got a soft spot for a lot of designers and high street stores, his favourite is Burberry, every time.

'It's not always about winning, it's not always about beating someone, it's about us establishing ourselves in the marketplace and having a career in music,' says JB, about how the group were thankful for all their success since The X Factor.

43

ORITSÉ

Oritsé calls his fashion sense 'sexy, cool, retro, different, unique, Oritsé!' And although he loves labels too, he knows that there's nowhere better to grab those one-off pieces of fashion than from Camden Market in London.

'Every element, from styling to sound to vocals, we did it with ambition, determination and dedication,' says Oritsé. 'We became an unshakeable force from the beginning.'

45

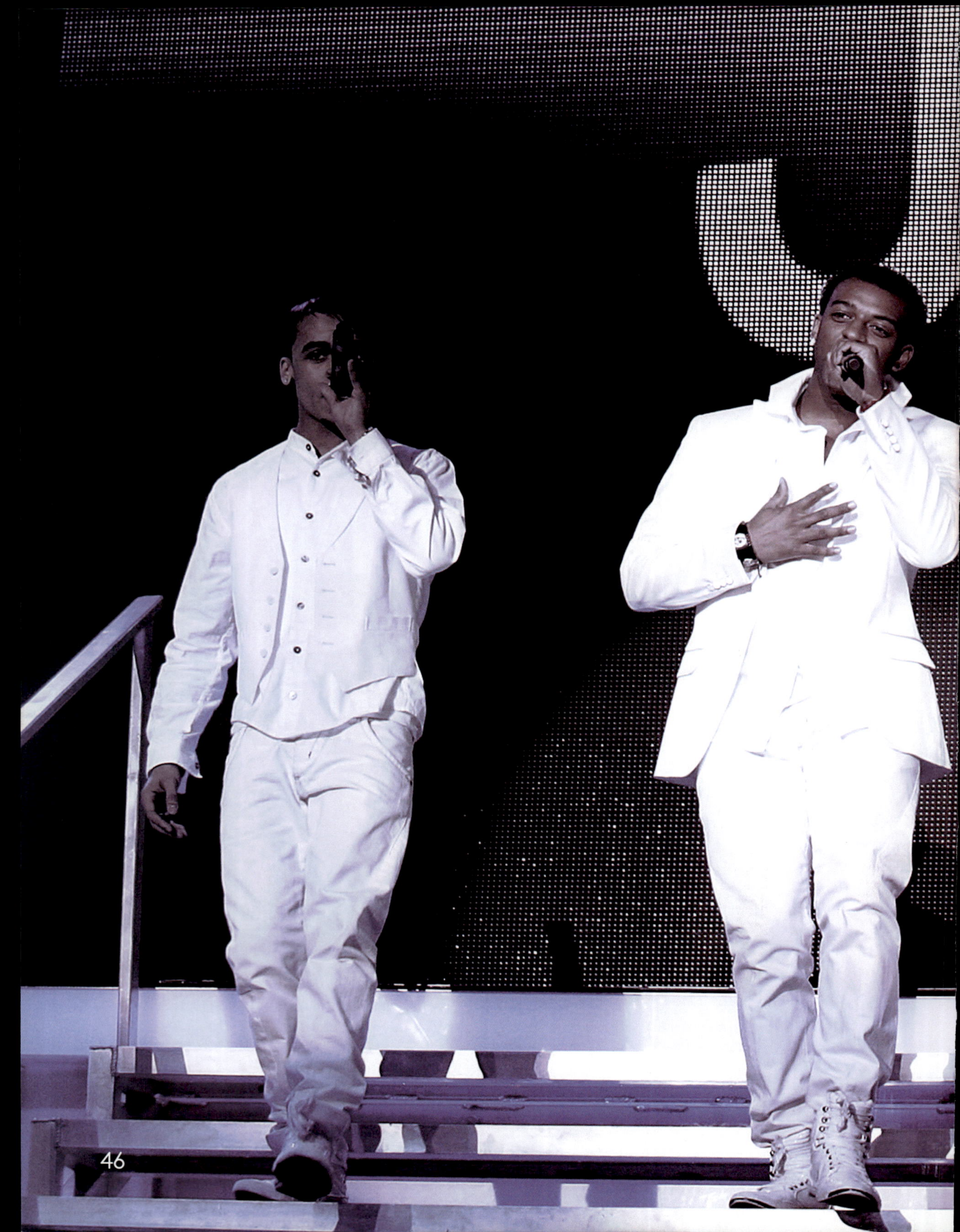

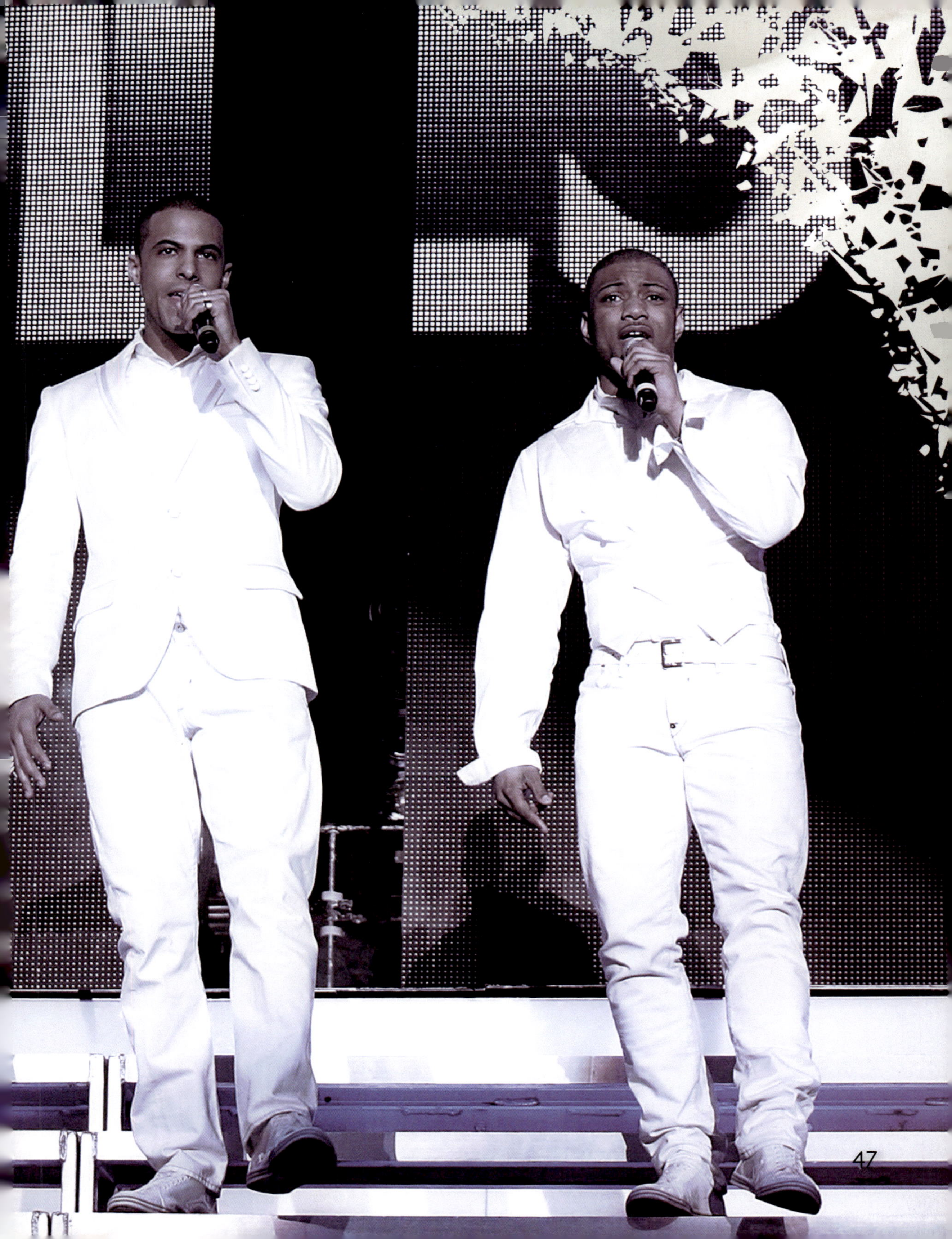

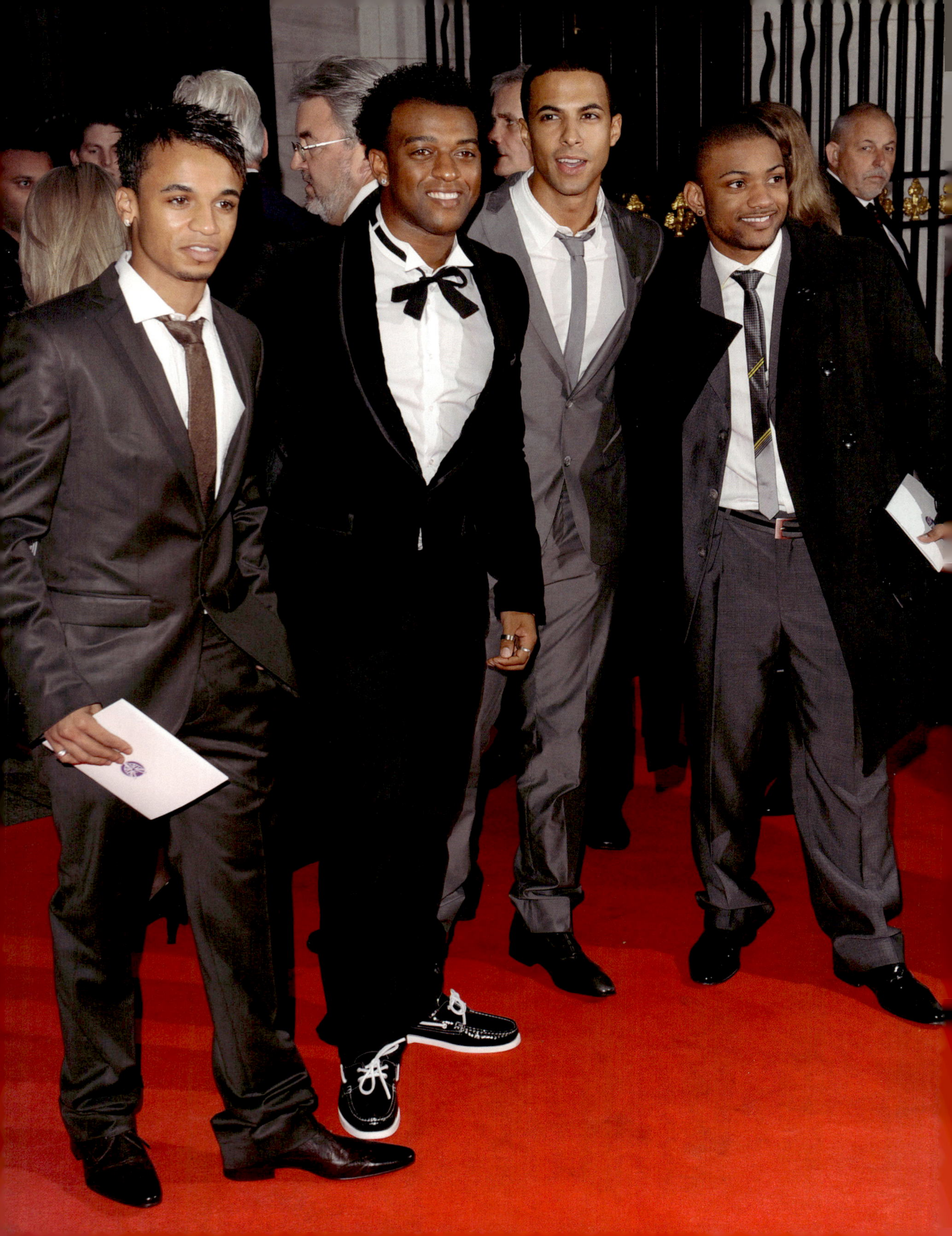

chapter 6

Romance

The boys started receiving fan mail when they were on *The X Factor*, but it was the fans outside the studio who presented them with the weirdest gifts. 'We've had charm bracelets, a dance DVD, lollipops, jumpers and a money box!' said Aston.

Romance and Rumours

If you believed everything you read in the papers, you would think all the boys must be romantically linked to every woman they stand within ten feet of!

In reality, the boys live a much more restrained life. When they formed as a group, they made a commitment to their careers that, unfortunately, meant that they had to break up with their long term girlfriends.

But as soon as they were performing on *The X Factor* they wasted no time in attracting potential girlfriends. They started working out every day, and even stripped off for a raunchy photoshoot in *Heat* magazine!

But having dedicated so much time to their careers meant the boys just didn't have time to find girlfriends, regardless of how tight their six packs may be!

So, while they were on *The X Factor*, they signed up for speed dating sessions! The hunky boys had been warned by protective mentor Cheryl Cole that they better keep their eyes off her mentees, Diana Vickers and Alex Burke. But we can all rest easy – although they had a lot of fun, none of the boys found girlfriends through speed dating. Phew!

51

★ JLS

another beat

After the show finished, the boys were even busier, and had even less time to spend looking for girlfriends. That didn't stop them – particularly Aston and Marvin – being linked to new partners almost on a weekly basis. 'We all like to go out and have a good time, because we work very hard – but work comes first, not play,' says Aston.

But what about all those screaming girls? 'There are girls out there who will just chuck themselves at you for your status,' admits Aston. But the boys are careful to look after each other, and watch each other's backs.

You have to hand it to the JLS fans – those girls can really be persistent! One dedicated fan even risked suffocation trying to meet her idols – hiding inside a zipped bag, which she got a friend to leave at a hotel that JLS were staying in!

So although these may be some of the most eligible bachelors on the market, they're remaining single for the time being – because they're married to their music!

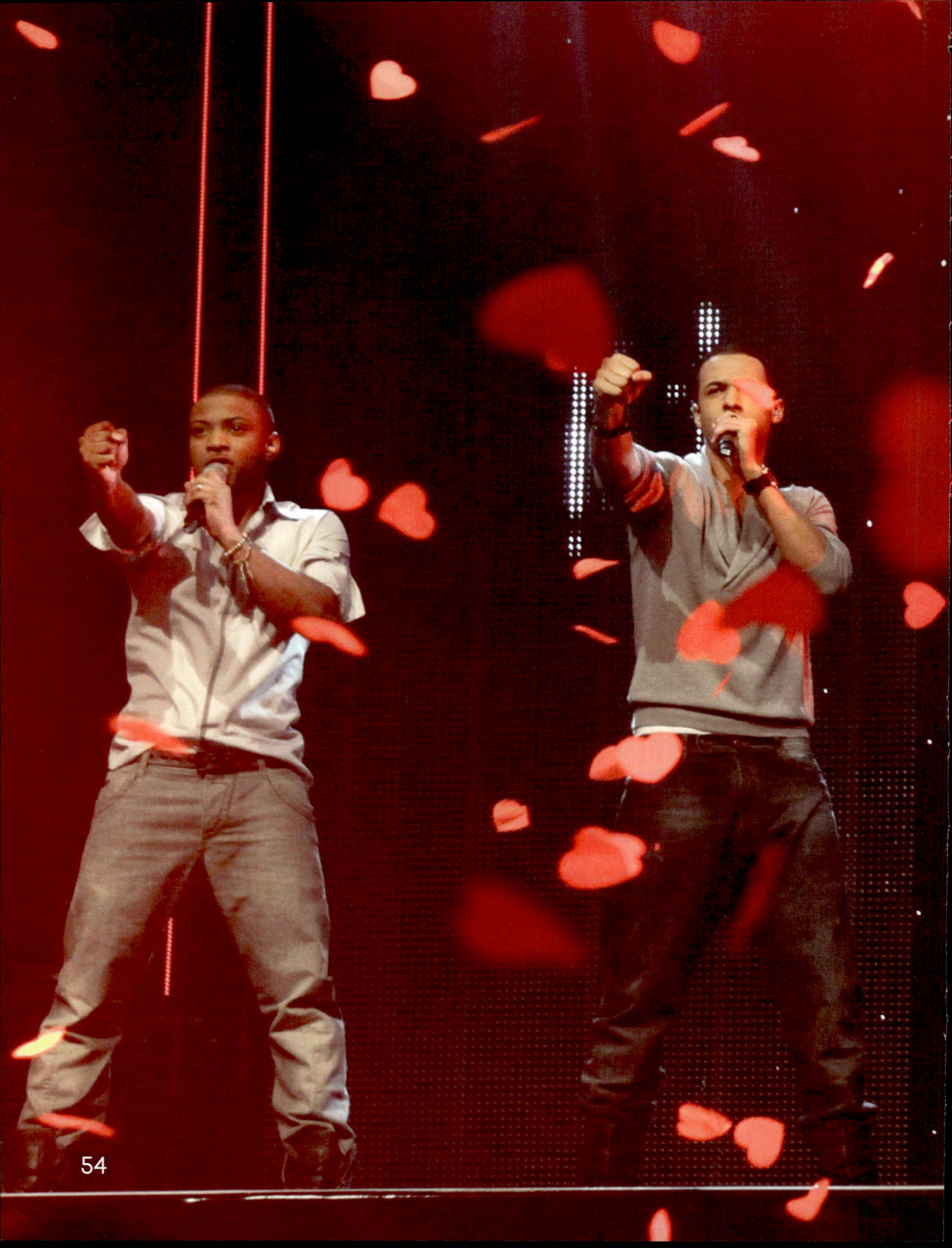

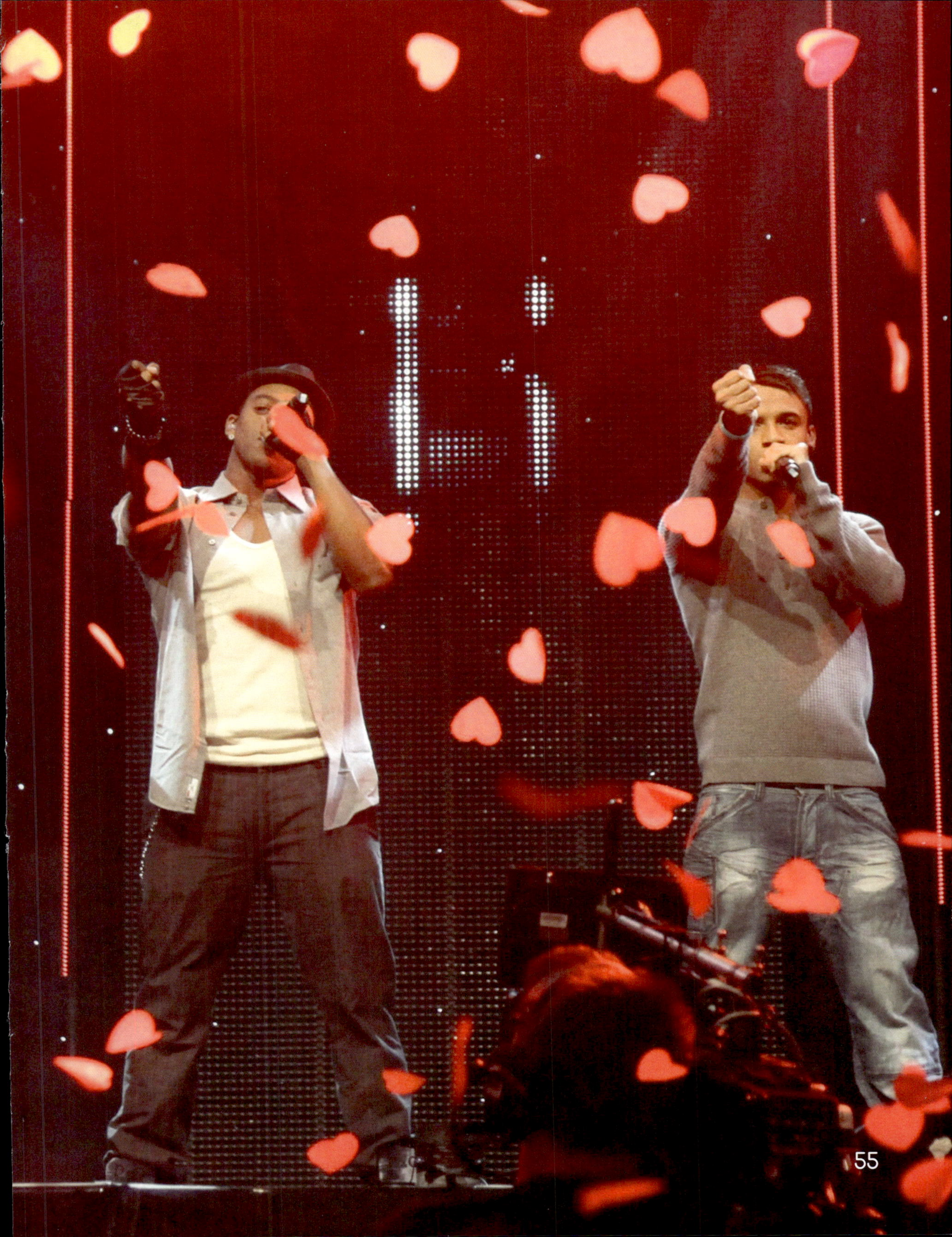

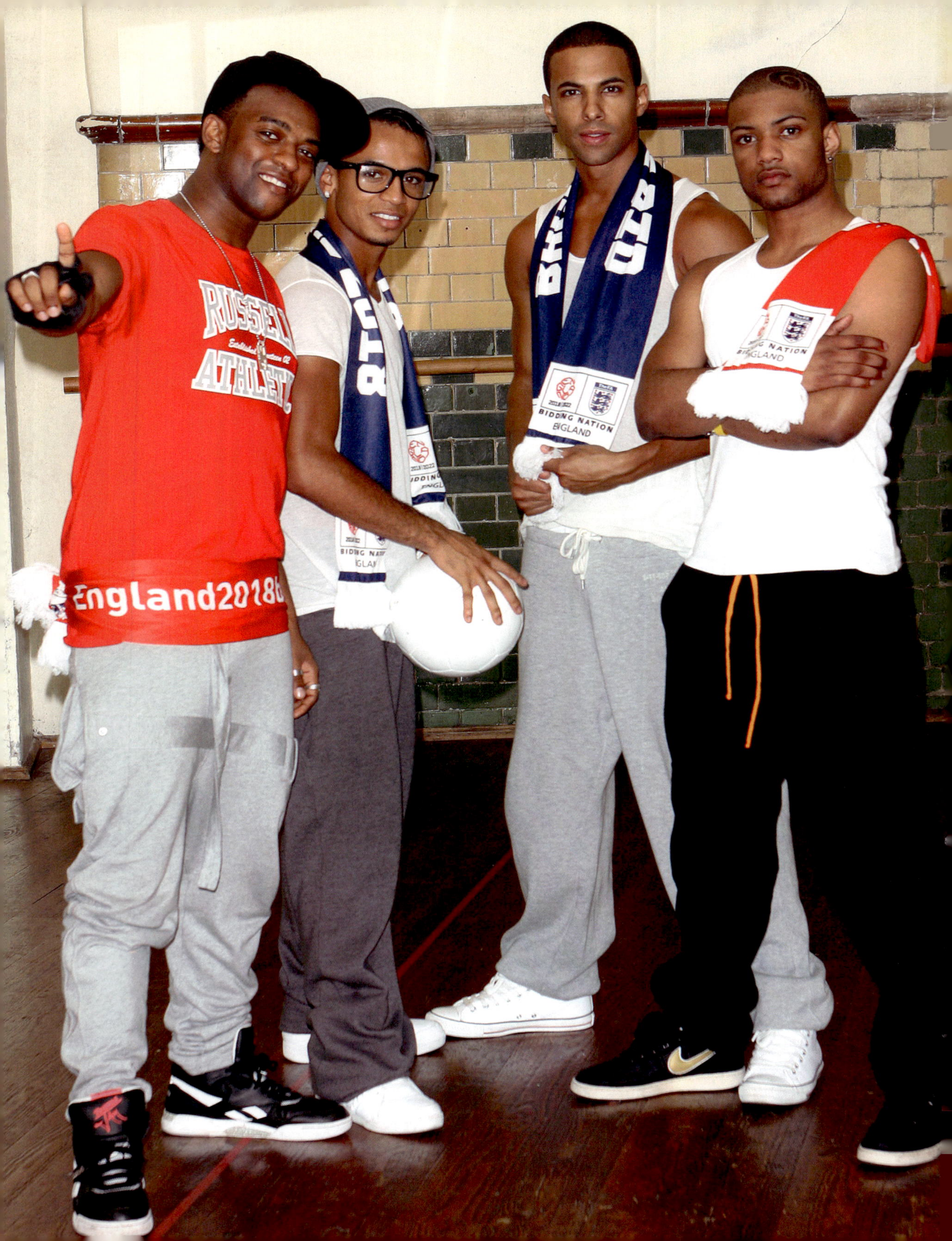
England2018
BIDDING NATION

chapter 7
The Future

Well, it's clear that Oritsé's dream of 'taking elements of the members of the greatest boybands of all time . . . and you'd end up with a supergroup' has come true – how could these guys get any bigger?

★ JLS

The boys have come so far in such a short time. It's a real rags to riches tale – four talented boys who found each other through Oritsé's masterplan, and have since become closer than brothers. They've managed chart success with hit singles, a platinum debut album, sold out arenas across the country, performed alongside some of the most famous urban artists around today, and even won top awards!

another beat ★

Keeping Both Feet on the Ground

You might expect some of this success to have gone to their heads, but the truth couldn't be further from that. These four boys heeded the advice of everyone they spoke to on *The X Factor* who told them to keep their wits about them and stay grounded. As a result, they've become more successful than any of them ever had dreamed of.

But the best thing of all is that the boys are sharing the most incredible journey of their life with each other, and with a shared ambition and love for what they do.

These four talented guys always knew they were destined for greatness, and they dared to dream. Just look where it got them! For these boys, the sky truly is the limit. Who knows what incredible things they will achieve next!

61

Picture Credits

Getty: 4, 5, 6, 16, 20-21, 25, 26-27, 30, 32, 33, 34, 39 left top and bottom, 41 bottom left and right, 43 top right and bottom left, 45 top left and right, 46-47, 59.

Rex: 9, 11, 19, 22, 24, 28-29, 39 right top and bottom, 41 top left and right, 43 top left and bottom right, 45 top right, 48, 50, 51, 52-53, 56, 58, 60-61.

PA: 13, 15, 38, 40, 42, 44, 45 top left, 54-55.

Acknowledgements

Posy Edwards would like to thank Helia Phoenix, Jane Sturrock, Helen Ewing, James Martindale, Viki Ottewill and Rich Carr.

Copyright © Posy Edwards 2010

The right of Posy Edwards to be identified as the author of this work has been asserted in accordance with the Copyright, Designs and Patents Act 1988.

First published in hardback in Great Britain in 2010 by Orion Books an imprint of the Orion Publishing Group Ltd.

Orion House, 5 Upper St Martin's Lane
London WC2H 9EA

An Hachette UK Company

10 9 8 7 6 5 4 3 2 1

All rights reserved. Apart from any use permitted under UK copyright law, this publication may only be reproduced, stored or transmitted, in any form, or by any means, with prior permission in writing of the publishers or, in the case of reprographic production, in accordance with the terms of licences issued by the Copyright Licensing Agency.

A CIP catalogue record for this book is available from the British Library.

ISBN: 978 1 4091 2245 6

Designed by Viki Ottewill

Printed in Spain by Cayfosa

The Orion Publishing Group's policy is to use papers that are natural, renewable and recyclable and made from wood grown in sustainable forests. The logging and manufacturing processes are expected to conform to the environmental regulations of the country of origin. Every effort has been made to fulfil requirements with regard to reproducing copyright material.

The author and publisher will be glad to rectify any omissions at the earliest opportunity.

www.orionbooks.co.uk